NORTH YORKSHIRE

Michael J. Stead

ALAN SUTTON

First published in the United Kingdom in 1992 by
Alan Sutton Publishing, Phoenix Mill, Far Thrupp, Stroud,
Gloucestershire

British Library Cataloguing in Publication Data

Stead, Michael J.
  North Yorkshire
  I. Title
  914.28404

  ISBN 0-7509-0227-2

Typeset in 8/10 Bembo.
Typesetting and origination by
Alan Sutton Publishing Limited.
Printed in Great Britain by
WBC, Bridgend, Mid Glam.

NORTH YORKSHIRE

North Yorkshire has much to offer the visitor. This collection of over
ninety colour photographs is devoted to the spectacular moors and
coastline, attractive towns and villages, together with the castles and
abbeys which are such a striking feature of the landscape. Among the
well known views there are also some lesser known surprises.

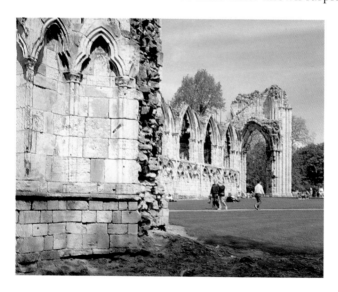

ARKENGARTHDALE

This dale is liberally dotted with evidence of the once booming lead mining industry, which was a major source of employment during the nineteenth century. Old engine houses or smelt mills such as this one still remain, as do the 'levels' – roughly bricked tunnels into the hillside, now in a dangerous state of disrepair.

ARNCLIFFE

Charles Kingsley described this valley, which he called Vendale, as 'a narrow crack cut deep in the earth'. Wordsworth visited and gave it the name Amerdale, which was later corrupted to Emmerdale for the popular television series. Many of the early episodes were filmed around this village green.

AYSGARTH FALLS

This series of waterfalls, Upp
Middle and Lower, are perha
the most famous location in
the Yorkshire Dales, and the
can be no more stirring sight
than to watch the River Ure
full flood, cascading over the
limestone steps that form its
bed.

BAINBRIDGE

Situtated on and taking its title
from what is probably the
shortest river in England, the
Bain, this was once the home
of the forest keepers appointed
by William the Conqueror.
One of their tasks was to blow
a horn each night during the
winter months to help guide
travellers safely to habitation.

BARDEN TOWER

Built by Henry Lord Clifford as
a hunting lodge, he actually
preferred to spend most of his
time here rather than at
Skipton Castle. Perhaps this
was because he was brought up
as a shepherd during the Wars
of the Roses, to protect him
from the Yorkists.

BOLTON ABBEY

The abbey was founded in
1154 on the banks of the River
Wharf by the Augustinian
order. Though much of the
stonework has been
requisitionéd over the centuries
for other buildings the nave
and aisle are still complete, and
are used today as the parish
church.

BOLTON WOODS – THE STRID

As the River Wharf flows through the grounds of the Bolton Abbey estate, it passes through a very narrow gorge. At its narrowest little more than a yard wide, this has gained a reputation as a challenging leap – but the width is deceptive and the rocks are slippery.

BOROUGHBRIDGE

The only reminders that this was a staging post on the Gre North Road are the old coaching inns. Its most famo landmark, however, is the Devil's Arrows, set in a field sandwiched between the tow and the bypass. They are in f Bronze Age monoliths.

BRIMHAM ROCKS

Formed originally some 300 million years ago, the layer of this millstone grit was first uncovered by glacial action, and then by the constant erosive action of wind and rain. Many individual rocks were given names by visitors, such as The Idol, Dancing Bear, and Druid's Coffin.

BROMPTON

William Wordsworth was married in the church here to a local girl called Mary Hutchinson, who lived at Gallows Hill farm above the village. Sir George Cayley, who lived at Brompton Hall and who has been called the Father of Aeronautics, invented gliders here long before the Wright brothers in America.

THE BUTTERTUBS

Situated near the summit of a
high fell road which links
Swaledale with Wensleydale,
these fluted cavities were
probably formed by the erosive
action of rain-water on the
limestone rock. They were
probably named by local
farmers, who used the cool
interiors to store unsold butter
until the next market.

BYLAND ABBEY

Moved from a site orginally
much closer to Rievaulx, this
independent community was
reputedly the largest Cistercia
church in England. It was a
refuge for Edward II from the
victorious Scottish army, but
led by Robert the Bruce, the
rampaging Scots eventually
ransacked the abbey.

CASTLE BOLTON

The castle was built by the Le Scrope family, which has had many illustrious members, including an archbishop of York, two chief justices, a chancellor, and five knights of the garter. Mary Queen of Scots was imprisoned here for some months during 1568.

CASTLE HOWARD

Across the lake lies the stately home of the Howard family, designed by Vanburgh. It contains many priceless treasures of china, antique furniture, and paintings by such great artists as Gainsborough and Canaletto. In addition to the lake, the extensive grounds also have magnificent gardens, ornamental waters, a mausoleum and obelisk.

COXWOLD

Shandy Hall, in this most southern village of the North York Moors National Park, was the home of Laurence Sterne, also the vicar of this parish. It was here that he wrote *Tristram Shandy*, the fi of the great classic English novels.

DANBY CASTLE

Standing on the slope of Danby Rigg, this castle looks more like a fortified farm. It was originally the seat of the Latimer family, and was also for a time the home of Catherine Parr, one of the wives of Henry VIII.

EASBY ABBEY

According to local legend these abbey ruins are connected to Richmond Castle by an underground tunnel. Many years ago a group of soldiers attempted to confirm this by sending a drummer boy along it. The sound of his drum disappeared somewhere between the two, and the boy was never seen again.

EGTON BRIDGE AND EGTON

Down in the Esk Valley is Egton Bridge, with the village of Egton beyond it high on the hill. Both villages date from before 1066. Egton Bridge is an area famous for its Catholicism, the massive and beautiful church of St Hedda perhaps more suited to a city than a tiny moorland village.

FILEY BRIGG

At the northern end of the quiet town of Filey, this mile long peninsula of rock snakes out into the sea. It forms a natural barrier on which many boats have come to grief. At low tide many interesting features can be seen, not least the strange rock formation itself.

FORGE VALLEY

Lying about four miles from Scarborough, the valley has been designated a national nature reserve. It is said to ha got its name because the mo from Rievaulx Abbey founde an iron forge here. The river running through the valley is the Derwent.

FOUNTAINS ABBEY

This was once the wealthiest Cistercian monastery in the whole of Britain, because of its lead and sheep interests. When it was surrendered to Henry VIII the inventory listed 2,356 cattle, 1,326 sheep, 89 pigs, and numerous horses. The buildings are still remarkably complete.

GARGRAVE

The village is quite a peaceful haven now, especially down by the river. It lies in the Aire Gap, which has been an important passage through the Pennine Hills since Roman times. It once had seven churches, but all except one were destroyed by Scottish invaders about 1314.

GLAISDALE – BEGGAR BRIDGE

As a young man Tom Ferris had to wade the river here to meet his love in secret, for his father strongly disapproved of the match. After making his fortune, Tom built the bridge as a token of his love, a symbol that all obstacles can be overcome.

GOATHLAND

Situated high on the moors the village may possibly have been founded by the Goths of southern Sweden, thus providing one theory for its name. The main feature of the village itself is the vast common land around which the houses are scattered.

GORDALE SCAR

Originally a cave system in which the roof collapsed, the eerie grandeur of Gordale Scar has been a tourist attraction since the eighteenth century. It has featured in the paintings of Turner and in poems by Wordsworth and Gray.

GRASSINGTON

During the lead mining boom of the early nineteenth century, this village was a major centre of accommodation for the miners, who travelled from the far reaches of the British Isles. Apparently it once resembled a Klondike gold rush town, with a similar degree of lawlessness.

GREAT AYTON

The young Captain Cook
moved to Great Ayton with his
parents when he was eight
years old. The graves of his
descendants can still be found
in the local churchyard, though
the cottage in which he lived
was demolished in 1934,
transported to Melbourne, and
re-erected stone by stone.

GROSMONT

A thriving iron and brick
industry here was responsible
for Middlesborough's rapid
growth as a street town. Now
the village is more famous for
being a terminus of the North
Yorkshire Moors railway,
which is run for tourists by
unpaid enthusiasts.

GUNNERSIDE

This village and the rest of
Swaledale typify the landscape
of the Yorkshire Dales. The
seemingly haphazard layout of
handbuilt rough stone walls
form the fields in which sheep
and cattle graze, away from the
barren heights.

HACKNESS

Almost hidden deep under a
blanket of snow in the
Derwent Valley, the village
church was founded in Saxon
times. A remnant of this early
house of prayer is preserved – a
cross complete with Saxon and
Latin inscription.

HARDRAW FORCE

This is the highest single drop
waterfall above ground in
England. Years of constant
erosion have formed concave
walls to the cove, so it is now
quite easy to walk behind the
torrent. The great Blondin
once crossed this chasm on
tightrope, stopping half-way
cook an omelette.

HARROGATE GARDENS

Bog Fields, or the Valley
Gardens as they are now
known, was a favourite place to
promenade after taking the
waters. Harrogate is now
internationally renowned for its
floral displays, and once a year
hosts a floral festival.

HAWES

One of the highest market towns in England, the tiny cobbled streets are a regular haunt for tourists. One of Hawes' most famous industries is rope-making, and it is also a distribution centre for Wensleydale cheese. Here also is the Upper Dales Folk Museum and the legendary Kit Calvert's Bookshop.

HELMSLEY

The castle soars over the market town. Originally begun in the twelfth century, the keep and curtain walls were substantially heightened in the fourteenth century, to ensure its impregnability against the Scots. The impressive defences were breached, however, during the Civil War.

HOLE OF HORCUM

Scientists say that this deep
hollow in the moorland was
made by a glacier, but locals
it was caused by a giant, the
Saxon King Wade, who
scooped up a handful of eart
to throw at his wife.

HOW STEAN GORGE

Over the centuries the How
Stean Beck has eroded its way
through the rock to form this
beautiful steep sided gorge. As
the beck cuts ever deeper it
leaves walls with carved
galleries. The discoverers of this
miniature grand canyon were
Victorian travellers, who
dubbed it 'Little Switzerland'.

HUTTON-LE-HOLE

The greens around which the cottages sprawl are kept immaculately cropped by the sheep which graze here. Their diet is supplemented in the summer months with titbits from the tourists, who visit primarily to meander through that superb time capsule, the Ryedale Folk Museum.

INGLEBOROUGH

Above Ingleton there is a vast limestone pavement, sparsely covered by a few trees. Within these minute canyons can be found many rare plants. The plateau is dominated by the peak itself, on the summit of which are traces of a Bronze Age fortified settlement.

INGLETON

This pennine village is a busy tourist resort, used particularly as a base by pot-holers who explore the many treacherous caverns under the limestone. For the more sedate visitor the main attractions are the Doe and Twiss Valleys, where there is a spectacular four mile walk along the riverside.

JERVAULX ABBEY

The gracious ruins of this monastery include these marble pillars which once supported the chapter house. Somehow they resisted the violent mob which ransacked the abbey after Adam Sedburgh, the abbot, died on Tyburn Hill. The monks here once produced what eventually became known as Wensleydale cheese.

KILBURN

Above the village there is a white horse, carved by the villagers. Unlike its southern counterparts, this has a limestone base rather than chalk, and so requires regular grooming. Kilburn was also the home of woodcarver Robert Thompson, whose trademark of a tiny mouse appears on every piece he carved.

KILNSEY CRAG

The most dramatic feature of upper Wharfedale is only about 170 ft high, but looks so spectacular because its top overhangs the bottom by more than 40 ft. It provides a serious challenge to rock climbers, many of whom can often be seen attempting this difficult ascent.

KIRKDALE MINSTER

This church is dedicated to St Gregory the Great, who was the Pope responsible for sending St Augustine to England. Perhaps the most notable feature is the Saxon sundial above the south door, the most complete example in the world. It shows the eight hours of the Saxon day.

KIRKHAM

Kirkham Priory reputedly was founded in 1122 by Walter d'Espec, in memory of his son who fell from his horse and was killed when his head hit a rock – supposedly the one that is now positioned in the main gateway.

KNARESBOROUGH

Below the town the River
Nidd wends its way through a
picturesque gorge, which has
many attractions. These include
The House in the Rock,
St Robert's Cave, the curious
Dropping Well, and the cave
where the soothsayer Mother
Shipton was born.

KNARESBOROUGH
CASTLE

The castle dates from the
twelfth century, though now
only this keep survives. The
rest of it was totally destroyed
by Cromwell's forces in 1648,
after a protracted siege. Earlier
in its history this fortress had
been a prison for Richard II
and a refuge for the four
knights who murdered
Thomas à Becket.

LASTINGHAM

The licensee of this inn was also at one time the local vicar, the profits from liquor sales intended to supplement a miserly stipend. Under the nearby church is a Norman crypt which is itself a complete church.

LEALHOLM

The infant Esk which cuts through the village provides on its grassy banks an ideal and safe setting for family picnics. It was also the home of John Castillo a woodcarver and Methodist preacher who also wrote poetry. This has earned him the title Bard of the Dales.

MALHAM COVE

Once, if local records are to be trusted, a mighty torrent of water fell over this cove comparable in height and grandeur to Niagara. Above the cove is a fine example of limestone pavements where the action of water has eaten into the rock to form tiny canyons.

MALTON

Situated by the River Derwent, this area has long held great strategic and commercial importance. There was a Roman settlement here, called Derventio, the walls of which were 10 ft thick! Today Malton is a thriving centre, its livestock market being one of the largest in the north of England.

MARKENFIELD HALL

Originally built around 131█
this fine old house is
surrounded by a moat. The
protection John de Markenf█
had intended did not help h█
descendant Sir Thomas who
like many other Yorkshire
Catholics, lost his lands and █
home during the Rising of t█
North some 250 years later.

MASHAM

This village is known nationally
through the Theakston
Brewery, which is responsible
for producing the notorious
Old Peculier Ale. Nearby, at
Ilton, is this folly, which was
conceived about 1820 by the
philanthropist William Danby
as a means of providing work
for local men during a time of
unemployment.

MIDDLEHAM

Middleham, now renowned for
its connections with horse-
racing, was once known as the
Windsor of the North, when it
was the home of Richard III.
The 'cross' in the foreground,
with its eroded Boar emblem
of the King, recognized his
granting of a twice yearly fair
charter to the town.

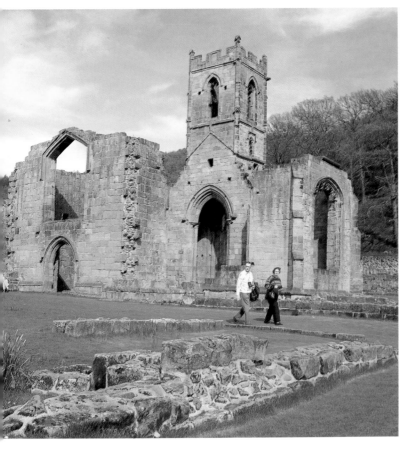

MOUNT GRACE
PRIORY

The remains of this fine old
Carthusian monastery date
from the late fourteenth
century. The monks who lived
here were bound by the strict
order of isolation and silence,
and the layout of the individual
cells and private garden areas
can still be seen today.

NUNNINGTON

Standing on the banks of the
River Rye is Nunnington Hall,
a part Tudor manor-house.
The beautiful gardens are home
to strutting peacocks, and
inside the house is a fine
collection of tapestries and
china. There is also a
magnificent doll's house.

NORTH YORK MOORS

Millions of years ago this wa
the largest tract of moorland
England – a fertile area with
network of large lakes. Whe
man inhabited it some 10,00
years ago it was still a
flourishing forest. The Moo
have burial chambers dating
from 5000 BC, and remains
Celt, Roman and Bronze A
settlements.

PATELEY BRIDGE

This place has been a market town since the fourteenth century, but its dramatic change in fortune occurred during the nineteenth century when the newly opened railway branch line not only increased the trade in stone, lead, and iron mined in the vicinity, but also made possible the advent of the tourist trade.

PEN-Y-GHENT

Rising above the Dales like a humpbacked whale, this is perhaps the most popular of the three main Yorkshire Peaks for the walker, even though it is the lowest. It is certainly the most dramatic and the ascent provides a challenging yet relatively safe scramble to the summit.

PICKERING

The town is built on a hillside, with the castle occupying the most prominent position. Legend has it that a king of the Britons lost his ring when bathing here, and that it was later found in the belly of a pike. Hence the place was called 'Pike o' Ring'.

RALPH'S CROSS

Many crosses on the moors have names and associated legends, but this is perhaps t best known. Erected in the eighteenth century by a loca farmer, wayfarers could leav donations in the hollow in t top, in gratitude of safe negotiation of the wild moo for the benefit of future travellers.

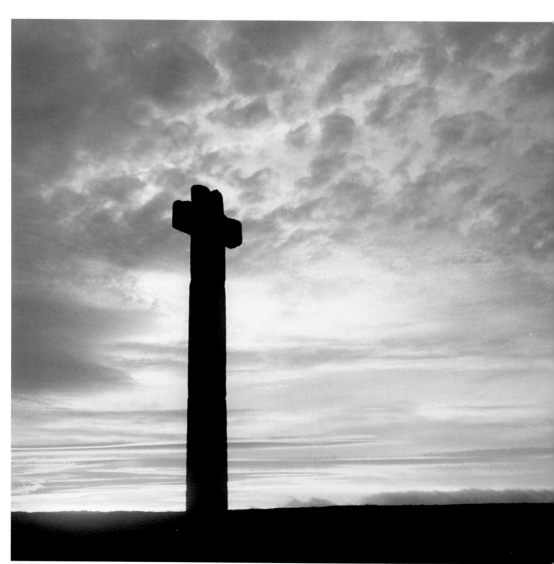

RIBBLEHEAD

The 24-arch viaduct is the most famous aspect of the Settle Carlisle railway line. When it was being built, this area was a vast shanty town housing the workers. The bleak landscape and a smallpox epidemic took their toll, as the memorial in Chapel le Dale church testifies.

RICHMOND

Dominating the town and the River Swale is Richmond's Norman castle. It has never been required to fulfil its defensive purpose. Beneath its walls there is said to be a cavern, where King Arthur and his knights slumber until England again requires their services.

RIEVAULX ABBEY

The abbey was founded in 1131, but actually took more than a century to complete. The community grew until thriving fishing, farming and woollen industry supported 640 people, and it had some 6,000 acres of land with 14,0 grazing sheep.

RIPLEY

In this village were billeted Cromwell and his troops after the Battle of Marston Moor, some fifteen miles to the east. On the church wall, bullet holes can still be seen where the Roundheads executed Royalist prisoners.

RIPON

Across the river, the cathedral
dominates the evening skyline.
It was founded in about AD 670
by Wilfred, Bishop of York,
and the crypt is one of the
oldest Christian structures in
England. The massive interior
of the cathedral was used by
Cromwell's forces as a stable
for their horses.

ROBIN HOOD'S BAY

Tiny cottages cling precariously
to the cliffside forming a maze
of narrow passageways and
alleys, each of which retains
many reminders of a once
thriving fishing industry. Today
tourism takes precedence, and
visitors may only enter the
village by descending the steep
main street on foot.

ROSEBERRY TOPPIN(

The hill is nicknamed the 'Yorkshire Matterhorn', referring to its shape rather than its height. Originally a conical hill, the discovery o ironstone ore led to shafts being sunk: eventually the whole of one side collapsed Though only just over 1,000 ft high, the views are exceptional.

ROSEDALE MINES

The remains of these kilns and similar ones across the dale are all that remain of the iron ore boom which took place in the nineteenth century. The railway trackbed now provides a superb horseshoe path for walking around the dale.

RUNSWICK BAY

Like most other villages on this part of the coast, the main enterprise now is tourism. The cluster of cottages, some whitewashed with flower bedecked gardens, provide safer accommodation since the sea wall was built, as the community was once very susceptible to both storms and landslips.

ST MICHEL DU MONTE

A chapel was first erected on this hilltop site around 1200, probably to provide a convenient prayer place for pilgrims, and also monks of Fountains Abbey when they were working in the fields. This structure dates from 1718, and was built by John Aislabie, owner of the Studley Royal Estate.

SCARBOROUGH CASTLE

The castle on its headland juts out dramatically into the North Sea, separating the commercial south bay from the more sedate north bay. Begun in 1136 by William le Gros, on the site of a Roman signal station, the fortress was not as impregnable as it appears. Most of its captures, however, were by ruse rather than violence.

SCARBOROUGH HARBOUR

Known as the Queen of the East Coast, this popular seaside resort has a long promenade and many tourist attractions, but its harbour still supports commercial fishing, and other cargoes such as timber and potatoes. Overlooking the south bay are Oliver's Mount and the Victorian Grand Hotel.

SEMER WATER

At night, there may perhaps be heard the ghostly sound of bells. For here, legend says, was once a golden city filled with greedy merchants. They turned away a weary and penniless angel, who in retribution called down a great storm, which flooded the city.

SETTLE

Lying under the towering limestone crag of Castleberg, the township has existed since Saxon times. A market charter was first granted in 1248. The Capital of the Dales is centred around this square, with the remains of the cross and the Shambles, a two tier arched building.

SHERIFF HUTTON

The imposing remains of the
castle built in the fourteenth
century tower over the villag
a landmark seen for many mil
across the Vale of York. It or
belonged to Richard III, but
now incorporated into the
neighbouring farm. Access is
no longer permitted, but the
castle can be seen from
footpaths nearby.

SKIPTON

The name of the town is a
derivative of Sheeptown, and
there is still a thriving livestock
market. Over the centuries
Skipton has been the home of
many different industries, many
relics of which can be seen in
the Craven Museum.

SKIPTON CASTLE

This castle is far more complete
than many of its
contemporaries, which is in no
small part due to Lady Anne
Clifford, who spent many years
restoring it. In 1659, she herself
planted the seeds of this vast
yew tree in the Conduit Court,
where spring water was
gathered in a basin.

STAITHES

Over the years many houses
have been swept away by the
storms which batter this coast.
One particularly violent sea
broke into the Cod and
Lobster Inn, where the waves
stole the entire bottled stock.
Scenes such as these cobbles in
Roxby Beck make the village a
popular haunt of artists.

STAMFORD BRIDGE

The mill, now restored, stands by the River Derwent. Nearby the famous Battle of Stamford Bridge was fought, in 1066. The Viking invaders were defeated, and their longship flotilla was sent scuttling back down the River Ouse.

STOKESLEY

Situated below the Cleveland Hills, the market town has a long wide main street, mainly of eighteenth-century appearance. There are many old inns in the town, and this area along the River Leven is tranquil setting for pleasant walks.

SUTTON BANK

Wordsworth stopped on Sutton Bank when travelling both to and from his wedding, to admire the views which on a clear day stretch as far as York Minster and the Yorkshire Dales.

THIRSK

This is a busy market town situated near the A19 in the Vale of York. The cobbled square is a major terminus for buses which serve the outlying rural communities. The town is at its busiest when the famous horse-racing meetings are held at the modern track here.

THORNTON DALE

The charm of the village gree
complete with stocks, and the
much bridged beck which
meanders across cottage
frontages, is undeniable, and
1907 Thornton Dale was vot
the prettiest village in North
Yorkshire. Many of its visitor
today sample the delights of t
now legendary ice-cream
parlour.

THWAITE

Dwarfed by the high fells all
around, this tiny village at the
head of Swaledale consists only
of a few cottages, a bridge, a
guest house and a shop. Yet
two shepherd's sons were born
here, who gained international
fame as naturalists and wildlife
photographers – Richard and
Cherry Kearton.

UPSALL

Lying at the foot of the
Hambleton Hills is the village,
which though tiny was once
deemed to be a town: the
house on the left was the town
hall. Why such a small village
should be important enough to
be given town status is lost in
the mists of time.

WEST BURTON

Tucked away off the main
Wensleydale road, many
people unknowingly bypass this
charming village, which has
one of the largest village greens
in England. Even those who do
discover it often miss one of its
most appealing features,
Cauldron Falls, which is only a
short walk along Walden Beck.

WHEELDALE

Stretching out for over a mile across the moor is the most complete section of Roman road remaining in the British Isles. The original foundations can still be seen, complete with a drainage system of ditches and culverts.

WHITBY ABBEY

The imposing remains of the abbey overlook the town of Whitby. It was in a building which was the predecessor these ruins in which lived the two most famous people associated with the abbey. They were Abbess St Hilda, who reputedly turned local snakes into stone and Caedmon, the father of Eng sacred song.

WHITBY HARBOUR

The harbour, abbey, St Mary's church, and below them the old dwellings of the East Cliff. Whitby has a long tradition of seamanship and shipbuilding, and has also been used by many famous writers as literary backdrops to their novels, among them Lewis Carroll, Charles Dickens and Bram Stoker.

YORK

Clifford's Tower was built to replace an earlier wooden tower. It overlooks the Castle Museum, which houses a remarkable collection of Yorkshire folk history artefacts, ranging from Victorian truncheons to farm implements and including three life-size street reconstructions.

YORK

Among York's eighteen
churches the Minster is
undoubtedly the jewel. The
largest church in England wa
begun in the thirteenth
century, though the site had
wooden temple as early as
AD 627. Its windows contai
some of the finest stained gla
in the world.